DECL YOUR LIFE

The Art of Tidying Up, Organizing Your Home,
Decluttering Your Mind, and Minimalist Living
(Less is More!)

KEVIN GARNETT

ERRORS

Please contact us if you find any errors.

We have taken every effort to ensure the quality and correctness of this book. However, after going over the book draft time and again, we sometimes don't see the forest for the trees anymore.

If you notice any errors, we would really appreciate it if you could contact us directly before taking any other action. This allows us to quickly fix it.

Errors: errors@semsoli.com

REVIEWS

Reviews and feedback help improve this book and the author.

If you enjoy this book, we would greatly appreciate it if you were able to take a few moments to share your opinion and post a review on Amazon.

For your convenience, here is a shortened link: **bit.ly/reviewdeclutter**

ENQUIRIES & FEEDBACK

For any general feedback about the book, please feel free to contact us at this email address: **contact@semsoli.com**

Table of Contents

INTRODUCTION..10

PART I: WHY SHOULD WE DECLUTTER?..........13

CHAPTER 1: DECLUTTERING – THE KEY TO
HAPPINESS...14

CHAPTER 2: TEN MEANINGFUL THINGS THAT
BRING REAL HAPPINESS..18
    1. Family
    2. Friends
    3. Doing Work That is Meaningful
    4. Thinking Positively
    5. Being Grateful
    6. Be Giving
    7. Be Forgiving
    8. Our Spiritual Beliefs
    9. Personal Freedom
    10. Health

CHAPTER 3: RECAP – PART I: WHY SHOULD WE
DECLUTTER...26

PART II: DECLUTTER YOUR HOME....................29

CHAPTER 4: DECLUTTER YOUR HOME –
WHERE TO START?..30
    Choose Your Day

Grade the Rooms
Decluttering Techniques
The 80/20 Rule
Making Up Your Mind

CHAPTER 5: DECLUTTER THE KITCHEN...........38
Keep the Benefits in Your Head
Some Clutter Is Inevitable
The Kindness of Others
Are You a Takeaway Hoarder?
Pots and Pans

CHAPTER 6: DECLUTTER THE MASTER
BEDROOM...44
How to Organize Your Drawers
My Secret Tip to Sort Your Wardrobe
Limit the Number of Items Allowed on Any
Surface

CHAPTER 7: DECLUTTER KIDS'
BEDROOMS...48
Kids Will Rebel
An Exercise in Mindfulness: Communicate
Your Priorities

CHAPTER 8: DECLUTTER THE LIVING
ROOM.........……...50
Use the Master Bedroom Approach
Tidy the Wiring
Store DVDs / CDs / Books on a Last Used
Basis

CHAPTER 9: DECLUTTER THE BATHROOM.....52
Clean up the Medicine Box
Take Out Any Gifts You Never Use

CHAPTER 10: DECLUTTER THE STUDY..............54
An Empty Desk = A Clear Mind
Be Thorough

CHAPTER 11: DECLUTTER THE GARAGE..........58
Where to Begin
Apply the Rules You Learned Earlier

CHAPTER 12: HOW TO KEEP YOUR HOME
DECLUTTERED...60
Establish a Routine
What's New?
Why Buy If There Is an Alternative?
One In - One Out

CHAPTER 13: RECAP – PART II: DECLUTTER
YOUR HOME…...42

PART III: DECLUTTER YOUR MIND....................67

CHAPTER 14: DECLUTTER YOUR MIND –
WHERE TO START? 68
Make Your Health a Priority
Identify Your Goals and Define the Path to
Reach Them
How to Get Started

CHAPTER 15: BE MORE MINDFUL.......................74
Mindfulness: Observe the Mind Clutter Without Judgment
How To Practice Mindfulness

CHAPTER 16: SPEND MORE QUALITY TIME WITH YOUR CHILDREN...........................80
Take a Piece of Paper and Write Down Your Daily Activities
Plan Quality Time With Your Kids
Forget Social Media: Be Social in Real Life!

CHAPTER 17: FIND FULFILMENT IN YOUR JOB...84
Practical Steps to Finding Fulfilment in Your Job
Ask Not What Your Colleagues Can Do for You, Ask What You Can Do for Them

CHAPTER 18: SHOW GRATITUDE FOR THE GOOD THINGS............................88
Why Practicing Gratitude Doesn't Come Easy
How You Can Practice Gratitude

CHAPTER 19: RECAP – PART III: DECLUTTER YOUR MIND....................................92

FINAL WORDS....................................94

DID YOU LIKE THIS BOOK?..................96

INTRODUCTION

Thank you for purchasing this book. It will help you to make a giant step towards improving your life, home and relationships; all benefits that decluttering offers.

Many of us today are trapped in a never-ending world of consumerism. Our houses are stuffed full of things that, if we are honest, we do not really want or enjoy. We then spend much of our emotional energy working out how we can sustain our life style, how we can afford the next unnecessary item, how we can manage our busy lives.

As a result, the really important things – our relationships with family and friends – suffer.

This book will help you to solve this very common problem. It will offer many practical methods of decluttering your home and your mind. It is not a book of theory. You and I both know that materialism has many negative connotations and do not need to expound on the many theories of this idea. It is instead a practical book which helps you to make the first steps towards decluttering, offering practical methods of completing the process and of sustaining the progress you will have made.

Another thing to note is that it this is *not* a book zealously supporting an entire lifestyle change to the detriment of those around you. It will recognize that we live in the conditions in which we live. That might include children, teens and partners. It offers ways to change, which considers the feelings of your loved ones.

What the book will bring about is a clearer, tidier, less distracting:

- **home in which to live, and**
- **mind with which to think.**

Read on, and by simply following the guidance inside see your goals reached, making everything better not just for you, but for your family and friends as well.

Decluttering is something many of us believe we should do, but most find it hard to make the first move. This book will help you to do that, and show that once you are underway, decluttering is much more straightforward than you might think.

Minimalism and decluttering are inextricably linked; this book will focus on the benefits of decluttering your mind and your home. In the process of doing so you will, if you wish, be following your version of a minimalist lifestyle.

This book is divided in 3 parts:

- **Part I: Why Should We Declutter?** In this first part, you will learn that decluttering your home and mind serves a higher purpose. If you are clear about your why, then the intrinsic motivation that comes from that will allow you to take action and accomplish everything you will learn in Part II and III.

- **Part II: Declutter Your Home**. In the next part, we're getting practical. You will learn how you can declutter your entire home, as we go from room to room.

- **Part III: Declutter Your Mind**. Decluttering your home is only one part of the equation. Real change only happens if we can also declutter our mind. In this last part, you will learn how you can take control of how you experience the world, taking out the clutter while keeping that which serves you.

I hope you are excited!

I am really happy to have you on board.

We have a lot to talk about, so let's get started, shall we?

PART I: WHY SHOULD WE DECLUTTER?

CHAPTER 1: DECLUTTERING – THE KEY TO HAPPINESS

It is a strange business, living in the world we have today. On the one hand, there is so much that is good. Medical care is the best it has ever been, and we are living longer, on average, then at any time in history.

In the Western and developed worlds, at least, there are:

- **good job prospects,**
- **relative safety from wars and natural phenomena, and**
- **it is safe to walk the streets. Mostly.**

We are not completely there with these advantages yet, but conflicts are restricted to certain areas, and we are slowly learning to cope with the horrors of earthquakes, hurricanes and so forth.

Employment is available to most, and transport facilities mean that almost every part of the world is accessible. The internet and other communication and technological advances mean that we can stay in touch with family and friends, wherever they are.

Yet for all the positives, all the advantages of living in the 21st century, **people's happiness is not especially high**. It is as though all the solutions offered by the world are creating extra problems left in their wake.

There are:

- Fears around security and terrorism.

- Outrageous acts of gratuitous violence, carried out in the name of religion, of politics, of racial purity and by deranged individuals, blight society.
- Climate change is a real and serious threat to the entire planet.

Who knows what conditions our children's children will be enduring in fifty years' time unless we take action, serious action, very quickly.

And we have worries closer to home. You may feel pressure to pay bills. Many of us feel pressured to keep up with the Joneses and be materially comfortable. There is the fear we have for our children, growing up in such a dangerous environment.

All of this is enough to send shivers of dread through our bodies – indeed, for many, it does!

What to do?

To get past these negatives we need, as always, to take a step backwards.

We need to:

- identify what is important to us, and then we must
- be clear about what we should do to achieve such valuable goals.

We need to see **what is stopping us from being the happiest we can** be and **throw out the trash from:**

- **<u>our homes</u>** and
- **<u>our minds</u>**.

We need to declutter.

We need to physically declutter our lives to allow us to become mentally clearer. We don't have to be Steve Jobs, or some equally wealthy member of the glitterati, to declutter. We do not need to have a home all in white. But we do need to take control of our own happiness and sense of well-being. We do what we need to to satisfy our own goals, and that is our version of minimalism.

CHAPTER 2: TEN MEANINGFUL THINGS THAT BRING REAL HAPPINESS

If there is a lot of clutter in our lives, we can lose sight of what really matters. Those things that warm our heart. The things that *make us feel alive…*

If our mind is clouded by a fog of clutter, we may mistakenly think that if we can only get that next shiny object, we will be happy. However, study after study shows that material wealth does not bring about real, long-lasting happiness. By decluttering our lives, both our surroundings and our mind, we create **space**.

With space comes **mental clarity**.
And with clarity, we open our eyes to see **the beauty that is all around us**.

So, before we dive into the do's and don'ts of decluttering your home and mind, let's consider for a moment why we want to declutter to begin with. Let's take a look at what we can focus a lot more on when we create more space in our lives: Ten meaningful things that bring real happiness.

You may not recognize yourself in every item on this list. But I'm sure many of them will strike a chord with you.

1. Family

We are, fundamentally, a tribal species. We like to be close to others. Contrary to many animals (although there are exceptions), we like to live in groups. Most animals bring up their young then leave them to live their own lives, probably never seeing them again once they depart. The role of the father in childhood is minimal, often reduced to the biological fertilisation of the egg.

That is not the human way.

Imagine for a moment saying goodbye to your son or daughter at age eighteen, certain you will never see them again.

Never meet your grandchildren.

Horrific.

When we look at it from a psychological point of view, our relationships with family fulfils two needs.
They:

- provide us with the social interaction we desire, and
- lead to personal growth – the notion within ourselves that we can become a better person.

As humans, we need physical touch. Yes, conversing online is better than not talking at all, but our bodies crave the intimacy of a hug. There is a biological reason for this. When we hug, our bodies release endorphins which give feelings of pleasure and satisfaction that cannot be matched by material wealth.

Try it.

Next time you see your partner, your children or your parents, hug them. Feel the warm tingle that is released, and know that they are experiencing exactly the same kind of sense of well-being!

2. Friends

Equally important in most people's lives are social interactions with friends. Family is great, but not every family member is necessarily your best friend.

Friends offer most of the same emotional benefits of family, especially when you become an adult. Friends satisfy the need for interaction and personal growth.

Largely, when we are with friends, we are happy. We enjoy chatting, hearing stories and sharing laughs.

3. Doing Work That is Meaningful

The first things that comes to mind when I say 'work' will be your job. But I mean it in a broader sense: it is not limited to paid work. It can include gardening, cleaning, cooking, playing with the children, playing a sports game or music. Any activity, in fact, that occupies us and gives us an emotional reward at the end.

Again, to clarify, for some people studying a set of data from a spreadsheet or writing a book about decluttering is as meaningful as working with the old or sick would be to another.

Meaningful work is defined as an activity which keeps us engaged, and which gives us challenges to complete. We feel a spike of pleasure when we net the basket in the sports hall, make the children laugh, finish a chapter or deliver a profit on a sale.

This is because we are psychologically wired to want to achieve our potential. Meaningful activities make us feel connected to the whole and help us to reach self-actualisation, in other words: helps us to achieve our potential.

4. Thinking Positively

Positive thinking is a key factor in people's happiness. Seeing the good rather than the bad, the positive more than the negative, the opportunity over the barrier.

Positive thinking is tough for many people. Because many of us, right from an early age, are placed in positions of failure; we are compared to siblings, fail in tests and so forth - we grow a defence mechanism that makes us fear the worse.

Failure to get that job was because of inherent bias in the panel, or that they do not like you. Negative thinkers do not see this failed interview as an opportunity to address weaknesses, as positive thinkers do, but as somebody else's fault or, even worse, because they themselves are inadequate. Thinking positively has a rippling effect on all aspects of life, especially in our relationships with family and friends. It makes us happier people, more fulfilled people. We turn into a person who thinks of what the future offers rather than what the past has denied.

There is a psychological concept called The Law of Attraction. Basically, what this idea says is that we surround ourselves with similar thinkers. Therefore, those who always see the worse are attracted to others who are negative. This group then spends much of their time feeling down and critical, and that reinforces the negative attitudes that prevail.

By contrast, positive thinkers will head towards others with a positive mindset. That group will then be creative, problem solving and takers of opportunity. They will feel positive about their lives, and that positivity is spread throughout the group, reinforcing the forward-thinking mindset they possess.

5. Being Grateful

There is an oft said truism that it is better to give than to receive. But better than both is to be thankful for what you have received. Think about it, when you are grateful you are recognizing that somebody else values you. They have taken the trouble to give a gift or a compliment specifically to you. There can be no greater boost to one's self esteem. When times are tough, and they are for everybody at some points in their lives, it can be hard to show gratitude. A good way of ensuring that you do, and that you can properly reflect on the reason for your gratitude, is to keep a journal where you list the reasons to be grateful.

6. Be Giving

A person who gives, whether physically or emotionally, is doing their best for others. Many psychologists believe that man is incapable of being completely altruistic. Even when giving, a motivation for doing so is the personal well-being a person feels as a result. And does this matter? Not really, because even if in giving you are gaining personal satisfaction, the recipient of your gift has the opportunity of showing gratitude.

A 2013 scientific **study** conducted by the University of Buffalo shows that caring about others creates stress resilience. How does this work?

One thousand adult Americans were asked the following two questions:

1. How much stress have you experienced in the last year?

2. How much time have you spent helping out friends, neighbors or people in your community?

The researchers checked the public records to find out who had died five years on.

The study results showed that every major stressful life experience increased an adult's risk of death by 30%. However, this was not true for those that also spent a significant amount of time helping loved ones and neighbors. In those cases, there was a **0% increase in risk of death**.

So, you actively build your stress resilience by caring about others!

7. Be Forgiving

Forgiveness sends a warm thrill through our bodies. We can almost feel the positive endorphins flow. Holding on to anger for another's actions is a negative emotion which ties us up inside, and keeps the negativity that evoked the act at the forefront of our thinking.

If somebody has gone out of their way to hurt us, then they succeed far more if we retain anger about their actions. But by forgiving, we reach out to another, we eradicate the anger from ourselves.

Like many other aspects in our lives, forgiveness is hard. It is not a feature imbued into us by our leaders and rule makers, for whom ambition is all and forgiveness is seen as a weakness. But then again, we can be better people than these.

8. Our Spiritual Beliefs

For most people, their religion is an important aspect of their lives. When life satisfaction is measured, it does not seem to matter what the religion is, or even if a person's beliefs are individual to them and do not link to a formalised religion. Simply holding beliefs, living a moral life, seems to be what is important.

9. Personal Freedom

Equally important for most people is their individual liberty. It is an essential factor towards their overall happiness. When we come later to looking at how we can declutter our minds to achieve the real-life satisfaction we all want, keep in mind personal freedom.

This could be your right to equality, to getting a job and to not be the subject of discrimination or abuse because of your gender, race or sexuality and so on. It could also be something much smaller than this. Perhaps the sense that your freedom is restricted by all you have to do, and therefore you do not have the time to participate in the things that are most important to you.

10. Health

You may be surprised that good health is only number ten on this list of meaningful things that bring real happiness. But last definitely does not mean least.

Health is taken as a given for many people. It is only when we start to deteriorate that we start to really appreciate physical health. This is something we will pick up on later, as we look at ways to declutter our minds. If we become unwell, then the fear and discomfort of this becomes a part of the clutter stopping us from achieving what we want, so we will need to look at ways of best ensuring that our health remains good.

CHAPTER 3: RECAP — PART I: WHY SHOULD WE DECLUTTER

Let's recap Part I: Why Should We Declutter. We saw that:

- The current world in which we live is full of contradictions — for example the best health support ever is matched by an underlying fear in our everyday lives.
- We are social creatures, and we are wired to get our pleasure from our relationships with others. Family and friends are most important within this idea.
- The things most important to most people are nebulous, linking to relationships and interaction with others. They do not relate to measurable wealth or material possessions.

In this first part, we have focused mostly on the things that make most people happy. Decluttering our mind is about getting rid of the things that get in the way of achieving what we really want.

By decluttering our home and mind, we create space. With that comes clarity. And with clarity, we can focus all our attention on the things that in our lives that make us feel connected.

The list of ten meaningful things that bring real happiness may be arbitrary, but I hope that most of them resonate with you.

Perhaps you noticed that the list did not contain any reference to financial wealth. No mention is made of material goods. Fulfilling work is important, but note that this relates to things that can be beyond a paid job, and there is no reference to monetary reward or climbing the ladder to the top. Although we need money to pay our bills, ultimately lots of it does not bring long-lasting happiness.

With anything in life, if we want to change it, we need to have a **strong why**. A reason that intrinsically motivates us to bring about change.

So, if you ever struggle with finding motivation to declutter your home or mind, please read Part 1: Why Should We Declutter again.

In Part II: Declutter Your Home, we will look at how you can create space in your home. This is essential if we want to be successful in cluttering our mind. But it is so worth it!

Here's an exercise I would like you to do:

- **Close your eyes for 1 minute**
- **Visualize a room in your home after you have taken out all the clutter. Can you see it?**
- **Now, bring your focus inward and become aware of your thoughts. How does it feel, being in this clean, organized room? How would you describe your state of mind?**

That's the power of decluttering...

PART II: DECLUTTER YOUR HOME

CHAPTER 4: DECLUTTER YOUR HOME – WHERE TO START?

This chapter will focus on practical tips to help you declutter your home. This is a great place to start your journey, because:

- it involves physical actions, and
- results can be seen quickly and, relatively speaking, easily.

As with all schemes, it is best to start with a plan.

Choose Your Day

A good place to start is to identify a day of the week, and a time within that day, when decluttering becomes your priority. Dipping in and out is much less successful, because the personal sense of achievement you get from starting in a messy, packed space and ending with it clear is harder to see.

For many, a good time can be when the house is empty and you won't be distracted by other people. However, everybody's personal circumstances are different.

Secondly, allocate a reasonable time for the task. An absolute minimum of two hours per session is needed, three or four is a better figure. You need to have enough time to make some progress. We all know that when clearing out, there tends to be a short period of additional mess, and nobody wants to end their session with a worse look than when they started – that would be completely demoralising.

So, let's agree, for the purposes of this book, that you can manage two lots of three-hour sessions per week:

- One session will be enough to declutter smaller rooms, like the spare bedroom or study.
- But you will need two or three sessions for busier rooms, such as the living room or kitchen.

But that is fine. Simply divide these larger rooms into sections, and tackle one of these sections at a time.

Grade the Rooms

The next step on your journey involves grading the rooms and spaces on a one to five. On this scale, the numbers mean the following:

- #1 – this is a room that needs no decluttering. Everything is in its place, and there are no unnecessary and unwelcome objects.
- #2 – this is a room that you can live with. Decluttering is minimal, and it can wait.
- #3 – you have a mild sense of irritation when in the room. You are conscious that it is cluttered, and there are things that shouldn't be there.
- #4 – this is one over-crowded room. Getting through the door is starting to be a bit of a problem and just entering evokes a feeling of annoyance. You are conscious of your body tensing up and stress begins to surface.

- **#5** – where the original purpose of the room has been completely lost, and things are so untidy and packed in that finding what you are after is a nightmare, and usually impossible to do.

Once you have graded your rooms, set out an order to tackle them.

Start with a mid-range problem room where you can get the benefits of seeing results within a session. Build up to the toughest challenges. Save the easiest rooms for when you have a busy week and would like to cut back on your decluttering time.

Decluttering Techniques

There are many ways of doing this. Some advocate:

- moving everything portable out of the room,
- sorting it, and
- putting back what needs to remain.

I would like to suggest a slightly different approach though. I believe that the best way is to work logically through the room, or the section of it you are clearing. That way, if you do have to stop, or something comes up, at least the room is still livable.

A small purchase of some sturdy plastic boxes, in different colors and clearly labelled is a good option to take. The boxes should be as big as you can carry (full). You gradually fill them up until complete, then transport them to the appropriate part of your house for final sorting and storage or disposal.

The boxes should be labelled as follows:

- KEEP
- STORE
- RECYCLE
- TRASH
- SELL

The **KEEP box** is for things that are in the correct room and will be going back to their homes once you reach that stage of your clearing.

The **STORE box** is for things that you need to keep hold of, but are in the wrong place. When the box is full, transport it around the house, dropping off things in their correct locations.

There is a subset here, which are the sort of things that you have to store because you might need them later, such as bank statements and tax information. That sort of paperwork might go to your study, garage or loft, so you can find it in the unlikely event that you need it.

The **RECYCLE box** is for things that might still have some use for others, but not for you. So, for example, old shirts might not be good enough for keeping or selling, but could do a big favor as art shirts for the local school.

That jacket you bought but never liked might be a good bet for the local charity shop. The plastic trays you have collected determinedly but never used could be used as storage holders in the garage, or maybe go to the recycling depot.

. ↵ **TRASH box** is as it sounds, for things that have no further use to you or anybody else. All that awaits these sad little items is landfill or the furnace.

The **SELL box** is one you might choose not to employ. However, old toys, clothes, kitchen equipment and so on might be things that you can raise a little extra cash from selling at a garage or car boot sale. Equally, you might think it is not worth the effort, and instead send them all to the local charity shop.

A little warning or two – most of us find it hard to throw things out. A good rule of thumb is that if you have not used it/worn it etc., for a year, then it is probably not something you will use again.

Also, objects promote memories, and time can quickly be lost as you think of those halcyon days of courtship the old scarf promotes in your mind. Be tough on yourself, or time will pass and little will have been achieved. When you sense feelings of nostalgia coming on, put the object into the KEEP or STORE box. You can come back to it later.

The 80/20 Rule

Many readers will have heard of the Pareto principle, better known as the 80/20 rule. According to this principle, 80% of the results come from 20% of the causes. This is true in business, in relationships and also if you want to declutter your home: we use 20% of our goods for 80% of the time, and the other 80% for only the remaining 20% of the time!

And that 20% use time may even be generous: many of our possessions are not used at all. So why do we keep them, cluttering up rooms, cupboards, drawers and wardrobes?

Studies suggest a mixture of reasons.

One is pure nostalgia. We do not want to throw away goods because they bring back memories that we want to retain. But photographs produce exactly the same effect, and take no space to store, other than on your phone or hard drive.

Another reason we hang on to things that we neither need or use is that we are, as a race, programmed to retain our possessions. It means that throwing things away becomes a conscious decision rather than an automatic act.

In many ways, that is a good thing since it reduces waste. But allied to it is our magpie-like instinct to collect. We therefore have to be firm with ourselves when we have no need of something.

Making Up Your Mind

So, there we are, faced with the STORE box (if the object made it that far) wondering what to do. There are some tips we can follow.

1. **Apply the 80/20 rule**. Use this rule, savagely: If it doesn't fit in the 20% of goods that make up 80% of your use, then you need to find a reason to keep the item, not a reason to get rid of it. If you can't come up with a reason, then it goes in one of the other boxes.

2. **The 'use-in-a-year' rule**. This is quite a generous rule for items that we do not need, and which are cluttering our house, and therefore our lives. If you haven't used it in a

year, then unless it has real sentimental value, or is an investment, it should go.

3. Ask yourself: **Does it fit in the category of life learning?** That pasta maker you bought. Fiddly to set up, time consuming and messy to use and the result was not a lot better than the fresh pasta you normally buy. Result? Back in the box and in the cupboard, where it has sat alongside the spare water filter machine and third juicer for the past two years. *You know what to do.*

4. **Is it still functional?** Most of us will find something, somewhere in the house, that no longer works, or is so out of date that it has no functional use. The giant laptop you purchased that has the memory capacity of an ill goldfish? The watch that came from the local shop, where the battery has gone and can't be replaced. The heavily chewed set of baby books that were given to you by that neighbour, with whom you never really got on. If it doesn't work or is not serving a purpose, why keep it?

The key point of this chapter is to have a plan. A plan for:

- working time
- the method of decluttering you will use, and
- to deal with those items that distract you from your task

In the next chapters, we will concentrate on practical tips for decluttering specific rooms. I will offer a number of tips, on a room by room basis, to help you with the physical decluttering of the home, starting with the hub of the home, the kitchen.

CHAPTER 5: DECLUTTER THE KITCHEN

The kitchen is probably not the best room with which to start your decluttering process. It is perhaps the hardest room in the house to clear. You need a bit of speed and experience to build up to it.

However, it is a good place to start in this book because of the very fact that it is one of the hardest to tackle.

When you move homes, a decision to dismiss a house you are considering as your next dwelling is made very quickly. Some estimates put it at within the first twenty-five seconds. You see the street, see the outside and step indoors and if it is not right, then you know.

That is why tricks like creating the smell of baking bread, fresh coffee and vanilla are so important to real estate agents, as is having a tidy front garden and porch.

But if you are still open minded after those twenty-five seconds, the next biggest factor in your decision making is the kitchen. It is the heart of the home, the room in which you almost certainly spend most of your time. The place where the kids head when they get in from school.

It is a room as warming as apple pie, hot chocolate and special meals. That makes decluttering the kitchen tougher than in most rooms. But you can do it.

Keep the Benefits in Your Head

This is true of any decluttering task, but is especially important in the tough kitchen. Your decluttered room will be easier to keep clean; you will find what you need more readily, and you will get that feeling of satisfaction that comes with being in a room that's tidy and functional.

It can even be worth writing down a list of the benefits, and putting them in the room in which you are working.

Some Clutter Is Inevitable

It might be annoying, especially when bills pop through the letter box, but mail does come. Papers and take away menus are delivered. Car keys need to be left somewhere. The kids' school bags need to be deposited. Homework needs to be done. Used crockery needs to go somewhere (unless your family is so trained that they put their milk glass straight into the dishwasher.)

The chances are that all of this happens in the kitchen. And that is important. If you live alone, then perhaps you can sort out routines that mean none of the above clutters your kitchen, but sharing with a partner or family and your decluttering routine needs to take into account real life.

My best tip is to allocate a space in the kitchen – maybe a work surface furthest from the cooker or sink – that is for the deposits of papers, mail and keys. Give yourself five minutes a day and you will easily stay on top of that space. We humans love routine, so perhaps you know that the time when dinner is cooking and no longer needs your attention, is the point you tidy the 'communal' shelf.

Decluttering is different from coldness; you want your kitchen (and, indeed, the rest of your house) to be somewhere that your family and visitors feel warm and comfortable in.

The Kindness of Others

Rather like the pasta maker used to illustrate a point earlier, the kitchen is the place where we are most likely to find unused gifts, and impulse buys.

Yes, that food chopper produces the most evenly diced onions, but by the time you have:

- got it out of the cupboard,
- dusted it off,
- plugged it in,
- reminded yourself of how it works,
- and prepared the onion to be prepared, so to speak,

you could have got your knife out and done the job.

Yes, the juicer with the special tool for depipping pomegranates seemed a good idea, but your old one works perfectly fine and, when you think of it, nobody likes pomegranate in your house. So, it has sat in the cupboard, clogging up space.

Apply your 80/20 rule, and ask yourself when was the last time you used the device. If you don't have a reason to keep it, then it goes into the RECYCLE or SELL box.

Are You a Takeaway Hoarder?

Is this you? Do you carefully wash every take away tray, every jam pot and little plastic container that held your ready-made dessert? Do you store them away for the day little Johnny needs 160 foil trays and 250 plastic ones for his school project on Mars? You know, the one he will never be asked to do?

Probably it is, at least in part.

I'm not suggesting that you get rid of them all. An ice cream container can make an excellent tub in which to freeze the left-over portions on yesterday's lasagne. Silver foil trays make great holders to store nails and screws in the garage and small plastic containers work brilliantly for the drawer and cupboard tidies which we will talk about later. But you don't need too many of them.

Pots and Pans

You know the problem. Every hanger has its pot, and the bottom cupboard won't even close: it is so full of saucepans!

However, I have a good suggestion for decluttering your pots and pans. Firstly, take out of the equation any specialist pans you have, such as the crepe maker that you use occasionally. Then, with the remainder, keep the ones you use most up to the number of hob rings you have, plus one. It is always handy to have one spare, but no more than that. Four hobs equals five saucepans.

CHAPTER 6: DECLUTTER THE MASTER BEDROOM

Your bedroom is one of the most private areas of your house. It needs to feel relaxing, to induce calm rather than stimulate the brain.

We know that, for most people, a decluttered room does this best. The visual distraction of jam packed shelves is taken away, and there is less chance of the mind racing over what to do with the second alarm clock you have just been given as a present.

How to Organize Your Drawers

Starting with the drawers is a good idea, and there is a tip here which can be applied to any drawer in any room. That is to make a do it yourself drawer tidy.

You can buy ready-made examples, which are tasteful...and expensive. After all, a house might have forty or fifty drawers in various bits of furniture. Simply put together all those little boxes and containers you have accumulated over time, empty a drawer and then decide on the number and size of the compartments that you need.

Find the right sized boxes and away you go. It doesn't matter that the boxes are mismatched, because the inside of a drawer is out of sight. Mismatching also *does* look good to many people, being original and purposeful.

If you run out of little boxes and cartons, another way of creating dividers is to use strips of firm cardboard. Make little slits at the points where the horizontal strips meet the vertical ones, and the object you create will have a lot of strength and stability. It's just like being back in art class in school.

If a do it yourself approach does not appeal, there is still a compromise to be had. Cutlery dividers are very inexpensive, and fit in more than just the kitchen drawers. They will do the job extremely well. If you want to avoid the plastic look, simply line them with tissue or wrapping paper.

And think how much time and frustration can be saved by opening a drawer and finding exactly what you want, sitting there in its own little home, rather than rooting around in the messy collection of brushes, packets of tissue, costume jewelry, the odd book and bits of a manicure set that often make up the insides of one of these 'junk drawers'.

My Secret Tip to Sort Your Wardrobe

I also have a great trick for getting wardrobes sorted. It requires a little bit of discipline and a different way of thinking, but leads to a decluttered wardrobe where the 80/20 rule is exemplified.

Most people have some kind of order when it comes to their wardrobe. Perhaps clothes are color coordinated, or are kept in blocks of similar items, for example blouses or shirts then jumpers and cardigans.

The tip I'm recommending means storing on a last worn basis. As you take an item off and hang it up, or it comes back for storage from the laundry, hang it on the far left. Slide everything else along to the right. You can start from the other side if you prefer, I'm suggesting going from left to right simply because that is how we read a book.

Over a short period of time, all of the clothes that you wear regularly will be on one side of the wardrobe, and everything that just sits forlornly waiting for a day in the sun will be on the other. So, that cardigan you thought you wore quite often, in fact you don't. You have a perfect, visual guide to what can be removed, recycled or sold.

The same principle can be applied to shoes. Although it takes a little longer to move your shoes along a space compared to sliding some clothes hangers, you will soon see that most of your shoes are worn little.

Limit the Number of Items Allowed on Any Surface

After the cupboards and closets have been decluttered and organized, move on to other areas of the room. An excellent way of creating and maintaining order is to set a limit on the number of items to be allowed on any surface.

This doesn't mean neglecting the photo of granny you now need to tidy away. You can rotate the items on the surfaces, but just don't exceed the total you have set. So, granny's photo might not be out, gathering dust, all the time. But when it is, it has pride of place on your display so that you can properly appreciate it.

Decluttering isn't about getting rid of everything, but simply hanging on to what you need. But there are some rooms in the house where the concept of the declutter needs to be weighed heavily against other needs, and those rooms are the kids' bedrooms.

CHAPTER 7: DECLUTTER KIDS' BEDROOMS

Children, especially young ones, feel comforted by having their toys around them. They like a touch of clutter, it gives them security. These rooms may have to be parts of your house where a little bit tidy is the best that can be achieved.

However, there are lots of storage items that can be purchased. A large chest for cuddly toys as they go in and out of favor, or perhaps some hanging bags for these. Shelving for board games, and plastic drawers or boxes for toy cars and bits of Lego.

While it is a valuable life skill to teach your child to be organized, and a morally sustainable one to discourage a desire for material goods, kids are kids. They like to fit in with their peers, and that means having the right toys, the right clothes, even the right duvet cover and pj's.

Kids Will Rebel...

When they reach their teenage years, kids are pre-programmed to be rebellious. It is how they learn to set their own limits.

So that tidy kid of eleven suddenly becomes a large lump, leaving dirty clothes on the floor and tangles of computer wiring.

The child of Disney rarely exists. But then again, rather than rage against it, thank your stars that your child's way of rebelling is to leave a messy bedroom – there is much worse they could be doing!

So perhaps the kids' rooms are the spaces where you enter with trepidation, and do the minimum to keep the room workable.

An Exercise in Mindfulness: Communicate Your Priorities

Adapting to where you kid is at and meeting him or her halfway can actually be a great exercise in mindfulness. We can't always get everything we want if we care about keeping the peace.

But if you can communicate what matters to you most (remember the 20/80 rule!), you may be willing to overlook your kid not making his or her bed in the morning, or watering the plants every week.

If you can catch them young enough to come on board with the big clear out, then you are likely to make better, if slower, progress. Yes, they will want to share memories of every trinket they find, but they will also commit more to a declutter if they feel a part of the process.

CHAPTER 8: DECLUTTER THE LIVING ROOM

The living room is where you probably spend the majority of your waking hours at home. It's the room for relaxing, for sitting with your feet up and a glass of wine in hand. How much better to enjoy that with an organized, clutter free sight in front of you!

Use the Master Bedroom Approach

Similar rules apply here as were applied to the master bedroom.

Start with cupboards and drawers. Make use of your boxes, the ones labelled RECYCLE, TRASH and so on. Use drawer dividers to help with organisation.

 Keep at the forefront of you thinking that 'out of sight' does not mean 'out of mind', and every time you look for something, you will thank yourself for carrying out this declutter, and the ease with which your finding then occurred.

There are a couple of specific tips that apply to the living room.

Tidy the Wiring

First, your living room/living room tends to be a hotbed of wiring – for the TV, the sound system and so forth. Tidy this (safely). Buying a wire tidy is a good investment. Decluttering doesn't mean buying nothing, but sticking to only purchasing what you need. A wire tidy could well be one such item.

Store DVDs / CDs / Books on a Last Used Basis

Secondly, apply the same principle you used with your closet to your DVD, CD and book collection. You will soon see what you watch and play, and what is no longer to your taste. If you don't use it, don't keep it.

CHAPTER 9: DECLUTTER THE BATHROOM

Gleaming surfaces are what we want in this room. Not crusty medicine bottles whose contents exceeded their Use By date aeons ago.

Think about what you need in a bathroom. Have one example of these, and one spare in case you run out. So, your toothbrush in its holder, and a new one, still in its wrapper in the rack.

Clean up the Medicine Box

Clearly, go through all medicines. Test number one is: do we need it?

If the answer is a positive one, then check the date by which it should be used. Only if an item passes these two benchmarks should it be retained. Do though dispose of medicines safely.

Take Out Any Gifts You Never Use

The bathroom, after the kitchen, is probably the destination for well-meant gifts. You know, the pre-packaged perfume set that you will never use. Often, cupboards can fill up with gifts such as these, because people feel guilty about throwing them away.

But think logically:

- wouldn't most people appreciate their gift doing somebody a favour rather than sitting unused in a cupboard?
- Is there a charity shop that might appreciate them, helping them to raise money for a good cause?
- Or could you swap with a friend?
- Maybe a grass cut for two packs of perfume?

Follow the guidelines we discussed in **Chapter 4: Declutter Your Home – Where to Start**, especially the 80/20 rule and the 'use-in-a-year' rule.

Creative thinking will mean that your unwanted gift, currently cluttering a bathroom, ends up where it is wanted.

CHAPTER 10: DECLUTTER THE STUDY

A tidy and organized study is a real plus. It will make you more efficient.

Knowing exactly where the paperclips and staples are to be found will save time, as will knowing exactly where that tax document you need is kept.

More than this, there is a pleasure in entering a tidy and organized work space. It makes you anticipate getting jobs done. I hesitate to use the term 'look forward to…' but feeling productive makes the medicine go down, as least as effectively as a spoonful of sugar.

An Empty Desk = A Clear Mind

A tip for this room is to never leave work on your desk. Always either finish it, or file it for another day if you need more time. Work left on a desk makes for a negative start to a work session, and it distracts you as you consider whether to tackle the task you came in to do, or the one that is still sitting unfinished on your desk.

The Study is the room where you'll make some of the most important decisions in your life, especially if you work from home. You need mental clarity to make those decisions. As we learned in **Part I – Why Should We Declutter**, decluttering gives space, which results in mental clarity. So, removing the clutter from your desk really is a no-brainer.

Be Thorough

In many homes, the Study tends to become a room where we store random stuff that we don't really use that often. Some people even dry their laundry in the Study! To what extend you want to declutter your Study will greatly depend on what you use it for, and how often you spend time here.

If the Study is indeed a room where you:

- do your taxes,

- write that book, or

- do anything else that requires focused attention,

then you'll will want to have the same thoroughness as you apply with the kitchen, master bedroom and living room.

Use the KEEP, STORE, RECYCLE, TRASH and SELL boxes to organize all the stuff you have accumulated here over the years.

And then go through the items one by one:

- Is this item one of the 20% of goods you use 80% of the time?

- Have you used it at all in the last year?

- Does it fit in the category of life learning?

- Is it still functional?

At the end of **Chapter 3: Recap – Part I: Why Should We Declutter**, I asked you to do an exercise: closing your eyes, visualizing a decluttered room and checking in with your state of mind.

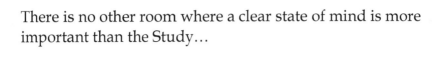

There is no other room where a clear state of mind is more important than the Study...

CHAPTER 11: DECLUTTER THE GARAGE

The big one saved for last. With 'garage', feel free to substitute 'loft' or 'basement'.

This is probably the most cluttered room in your house. It is where everything you are not sure what to do with ends up. You will need to be savage with your decision making. Do we really need the kids' push-along/ride-on car? Will it do anybody else a favor, or could we sell it?

Where to Begin

The very first declutter of this room might entail loading up the car several times with stuff for the waste disposal site, or hiring a van or skip. Don't worry, once it is done for the first time, it will be much easier to stay on top of.

The best way to start is to clear the big things so that you have a good space to work on. After that, make sure that you have shelving and or drawers. Large, plastic drawers are cheap to buy and do the job perfectly for a garage. They start at floor level, so are ideal if you are putting things away for the kids. A set of shelves above the height of the drawers adds an extra level of storage.

Apply the Rules You Learned Earlier

The same rules apply as to every other room, just on a larger scale. This is probably the space where most of the STORE box contents will end up, but still ask yourself:

- where it fits in the 80/20 rule, and
- whether you have used it in the last year

If the answer is 'no' to both, then you will need to find a reason to keep it, rather than find a reason to throw it away.

Use small containers and home-made drawer dividers to store things like nails and hooks.

Ask yourself whether you need the quarter tins of paint that are leaking away in a corner. What about the old tiles? The ones you saved because they were there when you moved in?

CHAPTER 12: HOW TO KEEP YOUR HOME DECLUTTERED

There you have it: you now know how to declutter every room in your home!

The first declutter will leave you feeling great. It will be like moving into a new home, as you rediscover space and clarity in your surroundings. Psychologically, you will know that it has been a job well done.

But how do you keep your home neatly organized and free of clutter?

It is definitely easier to stay on top of things following a major declutter. However, it still requires some level of focus and effort.

But don't worry, I have your back: these tips will help things from getting messy again!

Establish a Routine

The more people are living in your house, the harder it is to keep matters under control. The routine you established to start your process of clearing is one to keep up. Allocate an hour per week, not for cleaning, but for maintaining your declutter. Aim to cover one big room or two small ones per week.

Also try to engage other members of your family. Pe
could be a pocket money job for the kids, or a shared
experience with your partner. After all, they are gettii
same benefits as you!

What's New?

When you are thinking of buying something, ask yourself two
questions:

1. Do I need it?
2. Where will I keep it?

If either question creates a negative feeling in your mind, then
put your purse away.

The thing is, if you really need something, then you will find a
place for it.

Why Buy If There Is an Alternative?

Considering borrowing or renting when you need something
for occasional use.

For example, if you need a patio washer, you will probably
only use it a couple of times a year. If your neighbor has one,
ask to borrow it. You will almost certainly find that you have
something they need on occasions and a partnership saves
money *and* clutter.

ou want to watch that new film, rent the DVD or download it to your TV or computer. Your local library is a great, inexpensive source of books, DVDs and music. Or subscribe to a streaming service such as Netflix.

One In - One Out

A personal goal you can set for yourself is to only buy something if you, as a consequence, recycle another item. That really focusses the mind on what you need or really want.

It will save you money and at the same time help to keep your house clutter free. Decluttering is not about having nothing, rather it is about really appreciating the things you have. The money you save can mean that you buy really good quality artefacts, one that will last you for a long time.

CHAPTER 13: RECAP – PART II: DECLUTTER YOUR HOME

Before we move on to Part III: Declutter Your Mind, let's first recap Part II: Declutter Your Home.

We have looked at practical ways we can make our home a clearer, more defined and less cluttered place. You will gain enormous psychological benefits from living clutter free.

Apply these key tips to help you get rid of the unnecessary and maintain a home free from mess.

- The 80/20 rule; that we use just 20% cent of our possessions for 80% of the time.

- If we haven't used something for a year, then we probably aren't going to again. Get rid of it.

- Use labelled boxes (KEEP / STORE /RECYCLE / TRASH/ SELL) to help you with your major declutter, and also to help you speed up by not getting distracted by decision making.

- Use the left to right storage solution for clothes, shoes, DVDs and such like.

- Make drawer tidies to help keep them organized.

- Establish a routine, and stick to it, even after the initial clearance.

- Don't push it with kids, instead focus on what matters most to you.

- Don't feel guilty about getting rid of unwanted gifts. The giver will appreciate it more if their gift is used rather than sit in a store cupboard.

- Keep what you want, get rid of what you don't.

In the last part of this book, we will look in much more detail about the advantages of decluttering your mind, and your life. As with this chapter, we will offer practical tips to get you started, and help you to keep up with your good intentions.

PART III: DECLUTTER YOUR MIND

CHAPTER 14: DECLUTTER YOUR MIND — WHERE TO START?

Decluttering your house is a giant step along the causeway to clearing your mind. We must have faith in ourselves to eliminate the waste from our psyche, and we take the journey at a speed that is suitable and comfortable for us. Some people will dive straight in, for others the process is much more gradual.

In **Chapter 2: Ten Meaningful Things That Bring Real Happiness**, you learned that if there is a lot of clutter in our lives, we can lose sight of what really matters.

By decluttering your home, you will take a giant leap to feeling happier and more balanced.

However, decluttering your home is only one part of the equation.

To really gain the mental clarity that is a prerequisite for fully appreciating the beautiful world we live in, you will also need to declutter your mind.

How is it that some people that seem to have it all are still depressed, some even suicidal?

Because real change can only come from within.

We are very much affected by our surroundings, that's why we started with decluttering your home.

But now we move on to the real game changer: creating mental space!

Make Your Health a Priority

Before we dive in, I want to emphasize the importance of your health. Good health is often not a life goal…until it starts to go away. But physical and emotional health are essential if we are to achieve our decluttering goals.

We need energy, physical and emotional, to bring about change. Decluttering the mind will help with mental health. It helps you to concentrate on what is important, think positively and dismiss the myriad of matters that get in the way of your emotional well-being.

But physical health is important as well. We must therefore advocate the importance of diet and exercise your search for a decluttered life. If you are ill, everything slips away – your home, your relationships, your work.

Eating a healthy diet is good for you, and your family. The process of cooking gives great chances for quality time to spend with your partner or your children, as it is an activity that can be successfully shared. Or, you can be cooking while your children are working or playing in the kitchen. So, although it takes time in your day, it provides huge opportunities.
Exercise is the same. It can be about going to the gym, or jogging. That can be a social activity with friends. But equally as effective are regular family walks, enjoying the outdoors together.

So, with all of the suggestions that follow on how to declutter your mind, include time for exercise. The time will be well spent, and will reduce the risk of ill health damaging your decluttered life.

With that said, let's get to it!

Identify Your Goals and Define the Path to Reach Them

Decluttering is an extremely personal thing. Our goals are unique to ourselves, as is the order in which we seek to achieve them. But we must start with two clear objectives.

- First, we need to know what our goals are.
- Second, we need a clearly defined path to reach them. This path should be littered with specific milestones that we can tick off when we achieve them.

Some of you will already know exactly what they are seeking from the process of clearing their minds. Others will only hold a vague sense that they are unhappy with the business of their lives, perhaps with the lack of focus that they hold or a notion that things can be better.

For this group of people, a great place to start in identifying your goals is to **think like a child**.

Ask a youngster what they want to be when the grow up and you will normally get a very clear answer:

- Pop Star!
- Teacher!
- Fireman!
- Celebrity!!

You will notice that when they speak, it is always with exclamation marks such is the clarity of their thought. Such conviction. After all, it is obvious what they want to achieve, how could anybody fail to see it?

Back in the second chapter we saw the ten things most people want from their lives. If you recall, personal relationships with family and friends were at the top of the list. Then there were a number of factors around giving, gratitude and forgiveness. Health was not seen as a high priority life goal, until it started to go away. Wealth, career climbing, and material goods did not feature among the top ten must haves.

How to Get Started

A good starting point is to choose a few things that are most important to you. Once you have achieved these, you can head back to seek to address more goals. But decluttering is about simplicity, and more than just a couple of goals to deal with at one time can lead to complexities that make success harder.

You might even choose to achieve just one thing at a time, that is all down to you as you match up the power of your desires against the time that you have.

What follows in the next chapters are four different ways in which you can declutter your mind:

1. Be more mindful
2. Spend more quality time with your children
3. Find fulfilment in your job
4. Show more gratitude for the good things in your life

Of course, you can set your own goals, I'm sharing these merely to inspire you.

The idea here is to take the principles from the following chapters, and apply them to your own situation. We are all unique and not two people have the same challenges to face in meeting their aspirations.

CHAPTER 15: BE MORE MINDFUL

The #1 thing you can do to declutter your mind is practice some form of mindfulness.

A popular definition of mindfulness is **awareness of present experience with acceptance.**

We tend to live our lives in a mind*less* way:

- When driving a car, we're often elsewhere with our thoughts

- We ruminate on the past, and dream (or worry!) about the future

- I even know people who basically see their body as a means of getting their head into meetings!

If you are brutally honest with yourself: are you 100% present and focused on what you are reading **right now**?

Or are you, in the back of your mind, thinking about what to get for dinner tonight, or perhaps that hurtful comment you received yesterday from John?

This is all clutter!

The key to long-lasting happiness is seeing things *as they are*, rather than *how we wish things to be*. Mindfulness practices can help us with this:

Mindfulness: Observe the Mind Clutter Without Judgment

A mistake some beginners make is that if they practice mindfulness, they should have no thoughts whatsoever. And when that doesn't happen, they get angry.

This is a wrong assumption. Mindfulness is not about getting the thought-stream to stop. It's the nature of the beast: the mind is designed to secrete thoughts. If you get upset about that, you are only creating *more* clutter!

So, what does mindfulness help us to do? Mindfulness is about changing our *relationship* to the thought. The goal is to no longer *identify* with, or believe in, each thought that arises in our mind.

Often, a lot of the mind clutter we experience comes from identifying with a certain thought, and before we know it we're taking a ride on the emotional roller coaster. A simple thing like a colleague not greeting you in passing, can kick-start a trail of thoughts, such as:

- *"She's so mean, she hates me"*

- *"Did I say something wrong? I need to learn how to keep my mouth shut, I always says these stupid things. I'm such a weirdo..."*

- *"When I was at the gym the other day, the receptionist looked funny at me. I hope she won't be there next I want to work out"*

Does that sound familiar?

By practicing mindfulness regularly, you will be able to quickly catch yourself if this happens. You will probably still notice a reaction to that colleague not greeting you, but that thought won't take you for a ride. By simply observing it, you will be able to hold your judgment.

Often, there is a perfectly logical explanation for that person not greeting you.

- Perhaps they didn't sleep well.

- Perhaps they themselves are not mindful persons, and are just so preoccupied with their next meeting that they didn't notice you.

- Perhaps their partner just told them yesterday they want a divorce.

By practicing mindfulness, you take back control of your state of mind, and save yourself a lot of drama.

How To Practice Mindfulness

There are a ton of different mindfulness exercises you can choose from. I can only scratch the surface here. One thing they all have in common though is: accepting the present moment *as it is*.

The first exercise I recommend is a simple, yet very powerful, thought exercise. You can apply it in any situation.

Whatever the situation is, answer the following question: Can you do anything about it?

- **Yes**: then do it and don't worry.
- **No**: then don't worry!

Eazy-peazy, right?

Yet, you'll be surprised how much clutter you can remove from your mind if you habitually practice this exercise whenever you find yourself stressing out over something.

Another exercise is one that both helps train your focus and brings about a deep sense of calmness: breath awareness:

- **Sit comfortably:** You can sit on a cushion or on a chair, both are perfectly fine. Straighten your back, by imagining a string attached to the top of your head, lifting up you up. Consciously try to release any tension from your body. Finally, close your eyes.

- **Become aware of how you breathe:** Place your left hand on your heart and your right hand on your belly. Start with becoming aware of how the breath naturally enters the body and then leaves the body again. Where do you feel your breath? Is your belly moving when you inhale, or do you feel the expansion more in your chest area? Is the breath fast or slow? Whatever you observe, try not to judge or change it. Accept that this is how you are breathing in this moment.

- **Breathe into your belly:** Bring your awareness to your belly and breathe deeply into it. You do not literally breathe air into your belly. But if you breathe deeply, your diaphragm will push down your abdominal organs, causing your belly to expand. Feel how your belly expands as you inhale, and moves back in as you exhale. Make sure your exhalations are longer than your inhalations. This relaxes your body even more. A good ration would be 1:2. So if you inhale for 3 seconds, exhale for 6 seconds. Repeat for as you long as you like.

Practicing belly breathing on a regular basis activates the relaxation response and brings your body back to a resting state.

The wonderful thing about this breath awareness exercise is that you can practice it any time of the day! Even at work, or in your car.

One of the main things I hope you take away from this book is that *less is more*. Meaning that if you have less clutter in your life, you will enjoy life more. With less distractions comes more happiness.

Therefore, I'm only giving you two mindfulness exercises. Your mind may object. That's just the nature of the mind: it always wants more, and chase the next shiny object.

There are countless other mindfulness exercises you can find in books, video courses and websites. However, I challenge you to give the two exercises you learned in this chapter a serious chance.

Imagine you are digging a well to find water. You will stand a much better chance if you dig 10 meters deep at 1 promising location, than digging only 1 meter deep at 10 different locations…

CHAPTER 16: SPEND MORE QUALITY TIME WITH YOUR CHILDREN

Many of us live very busy lives, and as a result we don't spend enough time with our kids. Before you know it, they moved out of the house and you're like: *"Huh, what happened in those 18 years between her being a baby and now?"*

If you can be more mindful in your interactions with your kids, and also remove a lot of daily that's taking up head space, you won't be saying this when the apple of your eye moves out.

Take a Piece of Paper and Write Down Your Daily Activities

Work out how much time you are currently spending, concentrating only on the quality time. Those moments when you are actively engaged with your child, and all other distractions are out of the way. Write it down. You then have a clear target to exceed.

Next, and you will see this idea coming up time and again, write down a list of what you must do during your day. Let's say that you must get the children ready for school in the morning, you have to go to work, you must shop, you must cook, you must do the laundry and you must clean.

Write down, for each day, the time it takes to do each activity.

See whether jobs can be combined, or shortened. For example, how about getting shopping delivered? You can place your order when the children have gone to bed, and the delivery could also arrive after bedtime, or early in the morning.

Another case could be the work you bring home with you. Could you do that during the time that the children are doing their homework, with you all sitting together in the kitchen, working together?

Plan Quality Time With Your Kids

Now plan your days. You should find that there are big gaps where there is (almost) nothing scheduled. These will be excellent times to spend with your children!

The next question is to ask what that quality time might look like. And the great thing with kids is that they will soon let you know what they want from their new mummy or daddy time.

If the children are young, can you change your own meal arrangements so that you can have a bit longer for the bedtime bath or story?

Can your work arrangements be a bit more flexible, so you can plan days out? Ask, and you might be surprised. Most employers these days understand the importance of family life, and will want their staff to be at their best. To get both requires a little flexibility on their parts.

Finally, set a timetable. Week one could be changing your shopping arrangements, week two working together at the kitchen table, week three might be your first special day out. You get the idea. Small milestones that you can complete gradually.

Forget Social Media: Be Social in Real Life!

If you set it up in this way, it seems really easy to declutter your mind allowing you to concentrate on your goals. Of course, if it were, then everybody would do it. **The key is to focus on what is important**. Nearly every person under 35 in the US has an active social media account. That means constant interruptions from friends and marketers.

Just step inside a supermarket and the marketing men are watching you. They can tell, from your phone, how long you spend at the ice cream counter, whether you look at ready prepared meals or fresh ingredients. And they will target you accordingly.

Friends will want to keep you in touch with all their latest news. As it happens. But it wasn't that long ago that we lived quite happily with none of this. If it is story time with the children, turn your phone off. Having a cuddle on the sofa? Turn the phone off.

When friends contact you, suggest a coffee instead. We know that interactions that are face to face are better than in '280 characters or less' over a tiny screen.

Writing down what you plan to do, and then spending ten minutes at the end of the day recording the extent to which you have achieved your goals will help you to stay on track. It will keep the picture of what you want to achieve at the forefront of your mind, remind you how easy it is to do this, and also remind you of all that you have achieved.

CHAPTER 17: FIND FULFILMENT IN YOUR JOB

Another big one if you want to declutter your mind is finding fulfilment in your job. Ideally, you'll do something you are passionate about. However, in order to make a living, there also has to be demand for your passion and skills. I mean, if – hypothetically – I were to write a book about my passion for dogs eating a pizza salami, how likely would it be for you to buy my book?

See my point...

Your job may not be your dream job. However, that doesn't mean you can't get a lot of satisfaction and fulfilment out of it. A lot of clutter in the mind is the result of work-related stress. Seeing the glass half full instead of half empty can massively contribute to your overall happiness.

Practical Steps to Finding Fulfilment in Your Job

What actually makes us happy is doing something well. Let's take your current job and see how you find more fulfilment in it.

Identify the priorities that make it a success. This will almost exclusively relate to relationships. You get the best relationships with your boss by doing your job; with your colleagues by being friendly and supportive and with yourself by having a positive outlook.

Combining these will mean you become creative and problem solving. That will further the cycle of success you will create by following the objectives above.

Remember, you have other things in your life, some of which are more important. Clearly, you need to do the work for which you are paid, and do that to the best of your ability and with good spirits.

Taking endless work home and being up until the early hours makes you less efficient. It clutters the mind and distracts from your goal.

Rather, like with the example of finding time for your children, list what you do in a day.

See whether you can be more efficient:

- Is it possible to combine tasks?
- Can you use technology more efficiently? Bosses like self-starters who identify their training needs, if that is what you require.
- Are you doing work that should be delegated?
- Do you feel the place would close without you? If so, you are wrong. Nobody is indispensable. In fact, those that think they are often are the ones missed least when they move on.

By batching tasks, delegating tasks you shouldn't be doing, and using technology to your advantage, you are creating a lot of space. From that place, and the clarity it brings, you will be able to focus on high impact tasks and excel at those.

If you're doing what you're best at, and cut out the clutter, you will feel much better about yourself *and your job*. Plus, your boss will probably take notice too!

Ask Not What Your Colleagues Can Do for You, Ask What You Can Do for Them

Back to paper – plan you working day. Write down what you want to achieve, when you want to do it and tick it off when the task is completed.

- Can you do little things to make life better for your colleagues?
- How about bringing doughnuts on a Friday?

Remind yourself to take care to watch out for others. A kind word when somebody seems down, or an offer to take the pressure off when they are struggling, can really enhance your working relationships.

Are you grateful for what others do? Do you congratulate a person when they do their work well? Even the boss likes to be acknowledged!

Contrary to what you may have heard at the coffee machine, *he does have feelings…*

Finally, can you spot when negative feelings begin to arise and dismiss them? Remember the Law of Attraction – positive thinkers attract similar people; so do negative employees.

Again, a written list of when you have given thanks, and when negative thoughts have come to the surface can help you recognize the good and bad, and so dismiss the worse while enhancing the best.

Once again, the principle here is that your mind is focused on your goal. Here it was about getting fulfilment from your work. All the unrelated thoughts to this goal should be dismissed from your mind. Don't worry about the new assistant's creeping up to the boss, or that the Head of Sales abuses his position by always turning up late.

Unless it is your job to deal with this, then let others handle it while you concentrate on your role, doing it to the best of your ability.

CHAPTER 18: SHOW GRATITUDE FOR THE GOOD THINGS

You will be getting the idea by now. Identify what is great about your life, keep a written record of your successes (and failures) in your given goal. Keep it at the forefront of your mind.

When your child brings you their fortieth picture of you done in art class at school, don't smile vaguely, put it down without looking and get back to your laptop.

Instead, stop working, talk about the picture and pin it to the fridge with your child present.

If there is no room, ask him or her which picture it should replace.

Why Practicing Gratitude Doesn't Come Easy

Daily gratitude for the small things isn't something that comes natural to most of us.

Jack Kornfield, a well-known Vipassana meditation teacher once said: *"If you can sit quietly after difficult news, if in financial downturns you remain perfectly calm, if you can see your neighbors travel to fantastic places without a twinge of jealousy, if you can happily eat whatever is put on your plate, and fall asleep after a day of running around without a drink or a pill, if you can always find contentment just where you are, you are probably a dog."*

Ha!

We as human beings are handicapped with what's called a negativity bias. From a survival point of view, it makes a lot of sense. Those who mistakenly saw the rock for a bear survived, whereas the ones who assumed the bear was a rock did not.

So, our ancestors were the ones remembering every bad thing that had happened and spent much of their lives anticipating more trouble.

And now we are wired to do the same. For example:

- If you completed 10 things successfully today, but made 1 mistake: what do you think you think about when you go to bed?
- If your boss gives you a good review, but there is one area for improvement, which one sticks in the mind?

In our time, living conditions are much safer than those of our ancestors. But most of are still inclined to focus more on the negative than on the positive.

I have good news though: you have the power to change that!

How You Can Practice Gratitude

Practicing gratitude requires that acknowledge all that is going well in your life. This may seem obvious, but how often do you actually even notice that:

- you arrived safely at work?
- the sun shines
- your toast is crunchy
- your computer starts without giving an error

Here are a number of ways in which you can practice more gratitude in your life:

- **List the ways in which you show gratitude**. A daily gratitude journal is excellent for this.

- **Set yourself a target each week which you can achieve**. It might be for week one, a little prayer of thanks that your family is healthy. Or a reminder to yourself to keep your 'gratitude journal' up to date.

- **Practice listening with focused attention when you have a conversation**. It might be a challenge to always listen actively when people are talking to you. Often, we are just waiting for them to stop, so we can say what *we* want to say. Right? By listening actively, I mean giving the speaker full focus, not being distracted by other things going on, or by formulating what you are planning to say next while the speaker is talking. Good active listeners give concrete feedback with nods, and by repeating key words.

- **Be willing to really look at yourself**. When your partner seems disappointed by a response you have given, don't just assume they are being moody. Instead, analyze how you have responded, and what they might have been hoping for. (Then conclude that they are being moody!). And then take a moment to practice gratitude towards yourself, for the willingness to take responsibility for your own actions.

We are habitual creatures, and as the habit of offering thanks becomes imbued in you, it will become an automatic reaction.

CHAPTER 19: RECAP — PART III: DECLUTTER YOUR MIND

Mental and emotional decluttering is a positive rather than negative action. It means starting with a positive goal you wish to achieve, and removing everything that stops you from achieving it. The idea is very similar to decluttering your home. There, you were seeking to retain only what you needed or really wanted, and threw out everything that got in the way of that.

When you declutter the mind, the process is similar. Decide on what you want to achieve, what you *need* in other words, and dismiss everything that gets in the way of that.

Decluttering is about simplification:

- Write down the goals you want to achieve.
- Write a plan to achieving those goals, with clear milestones you can tick off as they are met.
- Keep a journal or a diary where you list your successes and failures, to remind you of the progress you are making and keep you focused on your main goal.

Practice mindfulness and gratitude along the way, and you will feel more fulfilled, connected and happier!

FINAL WORDS

I hope that you have found this book useful. The principles I wished to establish are that decluttering is about setting new goals. About writing down those goals, and keeping a record of your progress towards them.

It is about simplification. Getting rid of things that distract you from your goals. It is about a focus on what you really need and really want.

In Part I, we established that material goods and wealth are not the most important things in achieving happiness. One could even go as far as to say that excessive material items, actually, can get in the way of our happiness. The same goes for a fixation on money. There is nothing wrong with some money – it is important to have our basic needs met. But when it becomes our reason for living, for the status it brings and the goods it buys, it becomes a very poor substitute for happiness.

That is when we need to physically get rid of the excess in our house, to allow us to live without distraction. You learned how to do that in Part II.

Finally, by decluttering our mind we complete the circle and are able to return to a state in which we entered this world: a baby is born into this world with no mental or physical clutter.

Decluttering your home and mind may be a daunting task when doing it for the first time. But I promise you, it is worth it. And it will be so much easier to keep both decluttered after your first successful try!

Decluttering, I hope you will see, is about keeping priorities at the forefront of thinking, and dismissing that which is unnecessary.

If you are reading this, it means you have made it all the way to the end. Well done! This tells me you have what it takes to take control of your life and change it.

Now I challenge you to take action. Apply what you have learned about decluttering. And I have no doubt that you will feel a much happier person as a result!

DID YOU LIKE THIS BOOK?

If you enjoyed this book, I would like to ask you for a favor. Would you be kind enough to share your thoughts and post a review of this book on Amazon? Just a few sentences would already be really helpful.

You can search for it on Amazon, or go to:

bit.ly/reviewdeclutter

Your voice is important for this book to reach as many people as possible.

Here is the link again: **bit.ly/reviewdeclutter**

The more reviews this book gets, the more people will be able to find it and enjoy the incredible benefits of decluttering their home and mind.

Thank you again for reading this book and good luck with applying everything you have learned!

I'm rooting for you…

NOTES

Made in the USA
Middletown, DE
15 August 2018